A Book For Kids About Pandas

The Giant Panda Bear

By

Frances York

Disclaimer

All information in this book has been carefully researched and checked for factual accuracy. However, the authors and publishers make no warranty, express or implied, that the information contained herein is appropriate for every individual, situation or purpose, and assume no responsibility for errors or omissions. The reader assumes the risk and full responsibility for all actions, and the authors will not be held responsible for any loss or damage, whether consequential, incidental, special or otherwise that may result from the information presented in this publication.

We have relied on our own experience as well as many different sources for this book, and we have done our best to check facts and to give credit where it is due. In the event that any material is incorrect or has been used without proper permission, please contact us so that the oversight can be corrected.

Table of Contents

What's In A Name?

The Panda Bear is also known as the Giant Panda. Its scientific name is Ailuropoda melanoleuca, which means "black and white cat-foot".

The Giant Panda belongs to the bear family.

Physical Description

The Giant Panda has black and white fur with the body of a bear. It can be recognized by the black patches around the eyes and ears with black across its body, arms and legs.

The general appearance of the Giant Panda gives it some camouflage in its natural habitat of snow and rocks.

The thick wool-like coat keeps the Giant Panda warm in the cold climate of the mountains.

Size

Adults can grow to a length of 4 to 6 feet long. They can be 2 to 3 feet tall from the shoulders when standing on all four legs.

4

Their tail can be 5 inches long which is the second longest in the bear family. The sloth bear has the longest tail.

Adapted from flikr - cliff1066™.

Males can weigh up to over 300 pounds. Females are smaller at 170 to 280 pounds.

Panda Eyes

In China, the Giant Panda is sometimes called "bear cat" because unlike other bears which have round pupils, the panda's eyes have cat-like vertical slits.

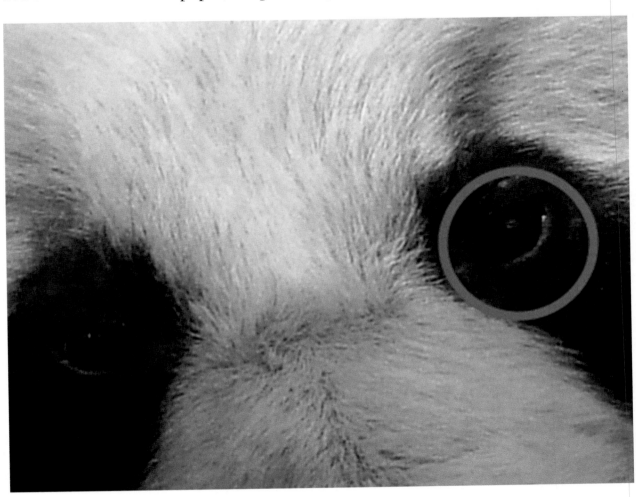

Adapted flickr - trespassers william. Some Rights Reserved

The Giant Panda's jaws have huge molars and muscles that can crush the toughest bamboo.

The Giant Panda's paws have five fingers and an extra bony stub that serves as a thumb. Sometimes called a "pseudo-thumb, the panda uses it to hold bamboo for eating.

History

In ancient China, the panda was considered rare and noble.

Geographic Distribution

Giant pandas use to roam wide areas in the lowlands of China. Their natural habitat has been getting smaller. The land has been taken over by farmland or destroyed by foresting and other environmental developments.

Adapted wikimedia – Joowwww

The Giant Panda's existence is being threatened with the loss of their natural habitat.

Today, the only place in the wild where Giant Pandas are found is in the mountain ranges of 3 provinces located in central-western and south-western China – Sichuan, Shaanxi and Gansu provinces.

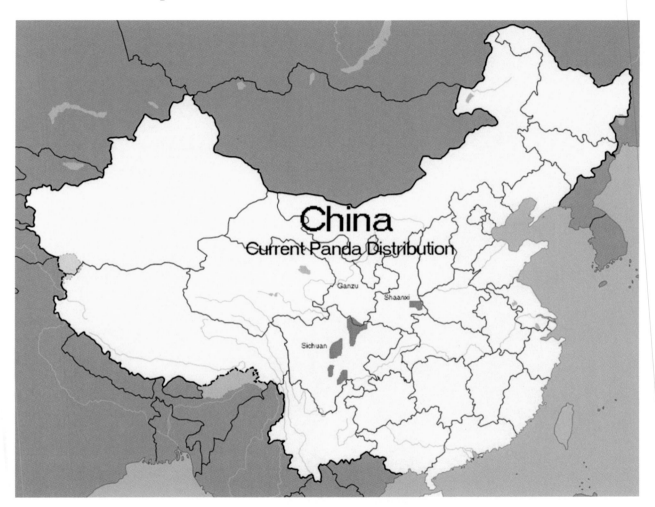

Adapted wikimedia - Joowwww

Habitat

The Giant Panda's habitat is found in the mountain ranges at elevations of 5,000 to 10,000 feet. The weather is constantly dense with mist and heavy rains. The area is usually covered in heavy clouds. Vegetation consists mainly of broadleaf and coniferous forests with a dense understory of bamboo.

flickr - Mark Knobil. Some Rights Reserved

Life Span

Pandas can live up to 20 years in the wild. In captivity they can live up to 30 years.

flickr - Matt Ryall. Some Rights Reserved

Behavior and Social Structure

Giant Pandas are territorial animals. As adults, they spend most of their time alone in the wild unless they meet for mating. They live on land only.

Giant Pandas can communicate with each other through sound, marking their territory with urine scent, clawing of trees or meeting occasionally.

Using their claws, Giant Pandas are good tree climbers. The trees offer shelter and safety.

Giant Pandas do not have permanent dens. Instead, they will roam within their territory, feeding constantly on bamboo. Because they do not hibernate, pandas will move to warmer areas during very cold months.

Pandas are normally gentle if left alone but may be dangerous if provoked. The Giant Panda is uniquely adapted to its environment.

flickr - omninate.

Diet

Giant Pandas eat mainly bamboo. They will also eat other things like grasses and meat from rodents, birds and other dead animals. In zoos, they get a diet that includes bamboo, sugar cane, rice, special high-fiber biscuits, carrots, apples and sweet potatoes.

18

How Pandas Eat

Giant Pandas normally eat in a sitting position. This allows them to use their front paws to grasp bamboo with their pseudo thumb.

19

Because the Giant Panda's digestive system is that of a carnivore like the other bears, it gets very little energy from eating bamboo. Special microbes in its digestive system help break down the cellulose from the bamboo and convert it into energy. Still, a lot of the bamboo that is eaten is passed through into the panda poop.

Adapted from opencage.info - David 1869.

That is why Giant Pandas are constantly eating. They can eat up to 20 to 30 pounds of bamboo a day. Because it eats so much, a panda will poop up to 40 times a day.

Why Pandas Look The Way They Do

Giant Pandas need to conserve energy because their food supply has such low energy value. They conserve energy by limiting their interaction with other pandas. They will also avoid going up steep slopes.

flickr - joelrivlin. Some Rights Reserved

The low energy diet of bamboo is also the reason why pandas have big round heads and round bodies. Animals with big round bodies tend to have a lower metabolism rate which helps the panda in conserving energy.

flickr - sanchez jalapeno. Some Rights Reserved

The round head of the panda is shaped by the powerful muscles in their jaws. Their jaws and molars are designed to crush and grind tough bamboo into finer fibres.

Food Source - Bamboo

There are a few species of bamboo available for the Giant Panda to eat. Each species of bamboo has a synchronous life cycle. That means the species will grow, flower and die together at the same time.

Because each species has their own cycle of growth, flowering and death, as one species is in the death stage, the panda will munch on another species that isn't in the death stage of its life cycle. So there must be at least two species of bamboo in different life cycles in the Giant Panda's habitat in order for the panda to survive.

25

The leaves of bamboo have more protein than the stems. When bamboo is scarce, pandas can eat meat from fish, birds, eggs and whatever it can find.

Water

The Giant Panda can get some of its water supply from the bamboo it eats. Bamboo contains half its weight in water. New bamboo shoots are made up of 90% water. For the rest of its water supply, the Giant Panda drinks water from the rivers and streams that are fed from melting snow in the mountains.

Scientific Classification

Before genetic technology became available, it wasn't certain whether the Giant Panda belonged to the bear family or the raccoon family. Newer technology has confirmed that the Giant Panda belongs to the bear family.

Adapted flickr - firstmac, flickr - Harlequeen. Some Rights Reserrved

Reproduction

Adult pandas gather together mainly for mating. Mating season is between the month of March and May. The female is able to get pregnant only once a year within a two to three day period in the spring. The male and female find each other using calls and scents.

29

Once mating is over, the male leaves the area. The female is left by herself to raise her cub. From the time the female becomes pregnant, she will carry the unborn cub for 95 to 160 days. The Giant Panda female can give birth to a cub every two years. An adult female will give birth from 5 to 8 cubs during her lifetime in the wild.

Baby Pandas

Baby pandas are called cubs. If two cubs are born at the same time, the mother will select the strongest club and leave the younger one to die. Because the mother can't produce enough milk to raise both cubs, by selecting the strongest one, this ensures a better chance of survival for the chosen one.

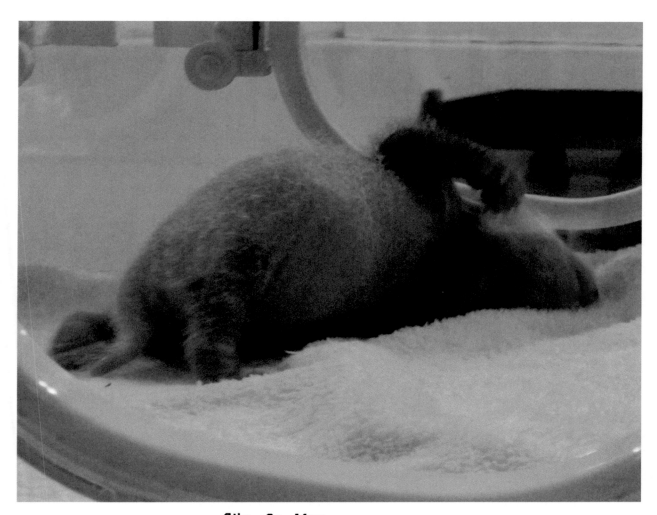

flikr - Su--May. Some Rights Reserved

The cub is born without sight and teeth. Its skin color is pink with a few short white hairs. It can weigh 3 to 5 ounces, about 1/900th of the mother's weight. A cub is completely helpless and relies on the mother for safety and protection.

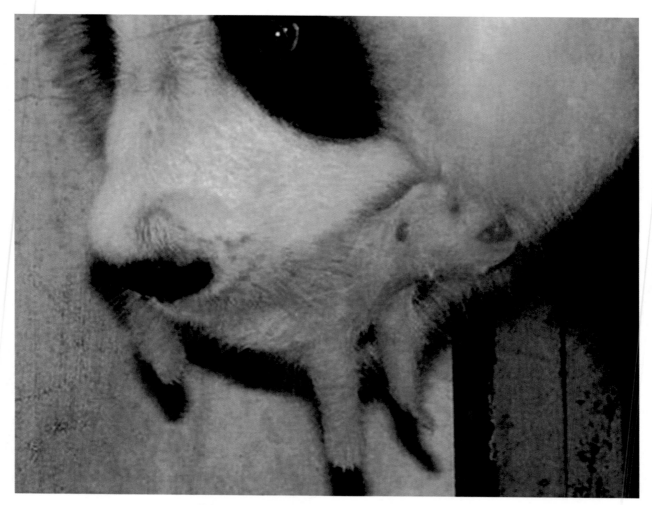

flikr - angells60640.

After 1 to 2 weeks, the cub's skin turns from pink to gray in the areas where black fur grows in. After a month, the cub will have the same markings as the adults. The eyes will open at 6 to 8 weeks. The cub will begin to crawl at 2 to 3 months. After 6 months, the cub will start to eat bamboo but will also continue to nurse up to 12 months. The cub will stay with the mother up to 2 years.

flickr — fortherock. Some Rights Reserved

Baby pandas become adults at the ages of 4 to 8 years. That is when they can start having babies. They are able to reproduce up to the age of 20 years.

What They Do For Fun

Pandas love to eat…

35

And eat…

And rest…

flikr - George Lu.

And eat.

Then they will sleep...

flickr - Pandora_60.

And eat some more.

Panda Diplomacy

In the 1970's, China began using the Giant Panda as a means to initiate diplomatic relations with the West. To foster cultural relations, pandas were loaned to Japan and America. This practice is known as "Panda Diplomacy."

flickr - scjody. Some Rights Reserved

In 1984, China began offering pandas on 10-year loans instead of giving them as gifts. Under the loan agreement, any cubs born during that time belonged to China. A fee of $1 million US is charged for the loan, half of it being used for conservation efforts to preserve the panda's natural habitat.

flickr - Su--May. Some Rights Reserved

Conservation Efforts

Due to illegal hunting and habitat loss, the Giant Panda is an endangered species according to the World Conservation Union's (IUCN) Red List of Threatened Species. Because of the panda's low reproductive rate, the population is slow to recover. Their numbers are less than 2,000 in the wild. There are about 300 pandas kept in captivity around the world in zoos or breeding programs.

flikr - fortherock. Some Rights Reserved

In the 1990's, several laws in China changed to allow the panda population a chance to grow. The laws introduced gun control and removed humans from living on the panda reserves. Although the numbers are increasing they are still rare. Some scientists now believe that there are around 3,000 pandas in the wild. According to a census, there were about 1,600 wild pandas in 2004. Conservation efforts and breeding programs have helped increase the Giant Panda's numbers in the wild.

Adapted from flikr - fortherock.

Thank You!

Thank you for purchasing this children's book. If you found it useful, please take a moment to leave a review.

Until next time.

Frances York

Image Attributions

13 flikr - Matt Ryall - Panda in enclosure
https://www.flickr.com/photos/mjryall/3631167953 - CC BY 2.0

14 flikr - puliarf - Joe Panda Kool
https://www.flickr.com/photos/puliarfanita/3009950334 - CC BY 2.0

15 flikr - George Lu - Panda
https://www.flickr.com/photos/gzlu/7708838248 - CC BY 2.0

16 flikr - Steven Belcher - Pandas
https://www.flickr.com/photos/8532914@N05/5594566074 - CC BY-SA 2.0

17 flikr - omninate - Giant Panda
https://www.flickr.com/photos/nate_kate/359678942 - CC BY 2.0

18 flickr - cliff1066 - Giant Panda (Ailuropoda melanoleuca) "Tian Tian"
https://www.flickr.com/photos/nostri-imago/3582031004 - CC BY 2.0

19 flikr- Kevin Dooley - Panda
https://www.flickr.com/photos/pagedooley/5402340884 - CC BY 2.0

20 Adapted from opencage.info - David 1869 - Giant Panda Ailuropoda melanoleuca
http://opencage.info/pics.e/large_11645.asp - CC BY-SA 2.5

21 flikr - joelrivlin - Baby panda
https://www.flickr.com/photos/joelrivlin/517628596 - CC BY 2.0

22 flickr - sanchez jalapeno - Chengdu Panda Breeding Centre
https://www.flickr.com/photos/sanchezjalapeno/6187560775 - CC BY-SA 2.0

23 flikr - timevanson - yun zi love bamboo 02 - San Diego Zoo
https://www.flickr.com/photos/timevanson/7824951306 - CC BY-SA 2.0

24 flikr - Augapfel - Looking through the Bamboo Forest
https://www.flickr.com/photos/qilin/491358938 - CC BY 2.0

25 flikr - kvn.jns - Bamboo Forest
https://www.flickr.com/photos/kj-an/3661499159 - CC BY 2.0

26 flikr - dalvenjah - bamboo shoots
https://www.flickr.com/photos/dalvenjah/336029756 - CC BY-SA 2.0

27 flickr - Marit & Toomas Hinnosaar - Mei Xiang
https://www.flickr.com/photos/hinnosaar/4711527255 - CC BY 2.0

28 Adapted flickr - firstmac flickr - Harlequeen
flickr - firstmac - IMG_8825-165.jpg
https://www.flickr.com/photos/firstmac/7423698056 - CC BY 2.0

flickr - Harlequeen - Raccoon Cute Pose
https://www.flickr.com/photos/harlequeen/491727233 - CC BY 2.0

29 flikr - Rick Weiss
https://www.flickr.com/photos/26049404@N05/5661740878 - CC BY 2.0

30 flickr - myglesias - Panda 1
https://www.flickr.com/photos/myglesias/418914949 - CC BY-SA 2.0

31 flikr - Su--May - Born Aug 16
https://www.flickr.com/photos/su-may/6142753329 - CC BY 2.0

32 - flikr - angells60640 - 4
https://www.flickr.com/photos/angells60640/3665571523 - CC BY 2.0

33 flickr - fortherock - Yun Zi - Baby Giant Panda - IMG_1683
https://www.flickr.com/photos/fortherock/4305507667 - CC BY-SA 2.0

34 - flikr - angells60640 - Thailand Panda Cub
https://www.flickr.com/photos/angells60640/3665601161 - CC BY 2.0

35 flikr-istolethetv - panda floss
https://www.flickr.com/photos/istolethetv/3703438542 - CC BY 2.0

36 flikr - fortherock- Panda Bear - San Diego Zoo
https://www.flickr.com/photos/fortherock/3898356265 - CC BY-SA 2.0

37 flikr - George Lu - Panda
https://www.flickr.com/photos/gzlu/7708863546 - CC BY 2.0

38 flickr - cliff1066 - Giant Panda (Ailuropoda melanoleuca) "Tian Tian"
https://www.flickr.com/photos/nostri-imago/3581217785 - CC BY 2.0

39 flickr - Pandora_60 - sleeping beauty
https://www.flickr.com/photos/77843769@N00/813075745 - CC BY-SA 2.0

40 flikr - cliff1066 - Giant Panda (Ailuropoda melanoleuca) "Tian Tian"
https://www.flickr.com/photos/nostri-imago/3582036252 - CC BY 2.0

41 flickr - scjody - Panda pile!
https://www.flickr.com/photos/scjody/4771024106 - CC BY-SA 2.0

42 flikr - Su--May - Cheng Du Panda Base
https://www.flickr.com/photos/su-may/6132305600 - CC BY 2.0

43 flikr - fortherock - Yun Zi - Baby Giant Panda - IMG_1499
https://www.flickr.com/photos/fortherock/4305495389 - CC BY-SA 2.0

44 & Cover Adapted from flikr - fortherock - Panda Bear - San Diego Zoo
https://www.flickr.com/photos/fortherock/3898365105 - CC BY-SA 2.0

Made in the USA
Lexington, KY
09 July 2019